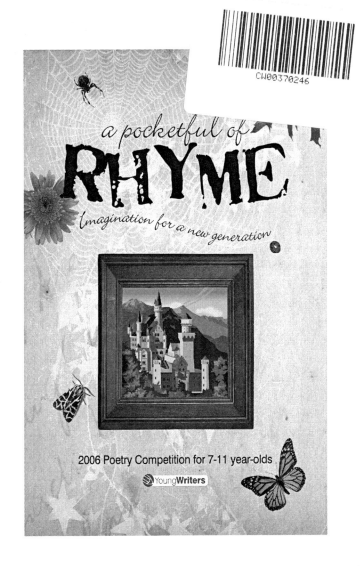

a pocketful of

RHYME

imagination for a new generation

2006 Poetry Competition for 7-11 year-olds

YoungWriters

West Yorkshire
Edited by Gemma Hearn

 Young**Writers**

First published in Great Britain in 2006 by:
Young Writers
Remus House
Coltsfoot Drive
Peterborough
PE2 9JX
Telephone: 01733 890066
Website: www.youngwriters.co.uk

SB ISBN 1 84602 563 X

Foreword

Young Writers was established in 1991 and has been passionately devoted to the promotion of reading and writing in children and young adults ever since. The quest continues today. Young Writers remains as committed to the nurturing of poetic and literary talent as ever.

This year's Young Writers competition has proven as vibrant and dynamic as ever and we are delighted to present a showcase of the best poetry from across the UK and in some cases overseas. Each poem has been selected from a wealth of *A Pocketful Of Rhyme* entries before ultimately being published in this, our fourteenth primary school poetry series.

Once again, we have been supremely impressed by the overall quality of the entries we have received. The imagination, energy and creativity which has gone into each young writer's entry made choosing the poems a challenging and often difficult but ultimately hugely rewarding task - the general high standard of the work submitted ensured this opportunity to bring their poetry to a larger appreciative audience.

We sincerely hope you are pleased with this final collection and that you will enjoy *A Pocketful Of Rhyme West Yorkshire* for many years to come.

Contents

Glusburn CP School, Keighley

Luke Phillip West (9)	34
Jack Fletcher (10)	35
Ellie Bolton (10)	36
George Albone (10)	37
Harry Eastbury (10)	38
Samantha Varela (10)	39
Shannon Roberts (10)	40
Daniel Davies (10)	41
Oliver Lewis (10)	42
Amy Beck (11)	43
Bradley Lyle (10)	44
Sam Abbey (10)	45
Benjamin Clarke (10)	46
Ellis Denton (10)	47
Laura Marklew (10)	48
Georgia Slingsby (10)	49
Harry Tosney (10)	50
Ross Hall (10)	51
Megan Duxbury (10)	52
Megan Moore (10)	53
Chelsey Reynoldson (10)	54
Fergus Briggs (9)	55
Sophie Nowell (10)	56
Jonathan Firth (10)	57
Mollie Guest (9)	58
Eleanor Ousby (10)	59
Sophie Thomas (10)	60
Daniel Jennings (10)	61
Alice Wild (10)	62
Lauren Boylan (10)	63
Adelle Edgar (9)	64
Zoe Atkinson (10)	65

Lady Elizabeth Hastings CE School, Thorp Arch

George Strachan (9)	66
Amy Tatterton (9)	67
Lois Saia (11)	68
Lucy Binsted (10)	69
Annie Hammond (11)	70
Emma Cook (10)	71

Sophie Hannington (10)   72
Daisy Ashworth (8)   73
Joanna Barnett (10)   74
Ellie Beanland (10)   75
Stephanie Jones (10)   76
Lochlan Shaw (9)   77
Laura Dunham (10)   78
Francesca Harrison (10)   79
Ben McGettigan (9)   80
Sophie Moncaster (9)   81
Harry Stobert (9)   82

Pool CE Primary School, Otley

Selina Stoves (9)   83
Claudia Cohen (9)   84
Evie Pedley (9)   85
Rachael Damp (9)   86
Beth Goldthorp (8)   87
Ellie Tempest (9)   88
Sam Hargreaves (9)   89
Daniel New (8)   90
Bevan Rainford (9)   91
Claire Mather (9)   92
Rachel Barnicoat (9)   93
Taylor Townsend (9)   94
Hannah Liles (8)   95
Jade Duncan (8)   96
Mark Claxton-Ingham (9)   97
Jack Jefferson (9)   98
Georgia Downes (8)   99
Lewis Fawell (8)   100
Jack Wood (8)   101
Zak Burke (9)   102

Ryhill J&I School, Wakefield

Rachel Hutchinson (10)   103
Charlotte Yates (9)   104
Annie Burgess (9)   105
Jennifer Cliff (10)   106
Charlie Schofield (9)   107

Wakefield Girls' High School, Wakefield

Hollie Joyce (9)	142
Lucy Booth (9)	143
Amber Balmforth (8)	144
Disha Shetty (9)	145
Siobhan McGrath (8)	146
Jessica Baker-Hollinworth (9)	147
Charlotte Maule (9)	148
Rosalind Hunter (9)	149
Stephanie Cheetham (9)	150
Jessica Johnston (9)	151
Georgia Houston (9)	152
Philippa Lister (8)	153
Emily Mappin (8)	154
Kristina Hall-Jackson (9)	155
Rimanee Kaur (8)	156
Emily Peace (9)	157
Costandia Demetriou (9)	158
Holly Clifton (9)	159
Umehra Khalid (8)	160
Eleanor Westwood (8)	161
Emma Cox (9)	162
Beatrice Marshall-Hodson (9)	163
Kathryn Marwood (9)	164
Moneek Chahal (9)	165
Amelia Dobson (8)	166
Evangelina Fozard (9)	167
Amy Rolinson (8)	168
Charlotte Lupton (8)	169
Jennifer Selim (8)	170
Jessica Holland (9)	171
Caitlin Halliday (9)	172
Claudia Lindley (9)	173
Kate Wilding (9)	174
Sneeha Lal (9)	175
Ellie Spruce (8)	176
Gemma Green (9)	177
Rebecca Jessop (9)	178
Lydia Jenkinson (9)	179
Rachael Dent (9)	180

The Poems

The Butterfly Poem

Butterflies like hiding in winter,
In summer butterflies bloom and flutter
Around in the morning air.

Butterflies glide softly around yellow,
Like the colour of my hair.

Fluttering around but when I cry,
The butterfly comes to me and makes me feel happy inside.

Butterflies softly glide all around
You will like to watch them they make you feel happy.

The butterfly can fly here and there,
The more I cry the more they fly,
And they hear everything I say.

Cody Davies (8)
Burntwood J&I School, Pontefract

The Butterflies

A butterfly flies high in the sky,
Their beauty makes me smile,
I watch as they dance by,
Fluttering their wings all the way.

Stepheny Lakin (8)
Burntwood J&I School, Pontefract

I Love Butterflies

A butterfly flies like a peaceful fly,
They make me happy all day long,
Fluttering silently, softly by,
Beat as the butterfly flies in the breeze,
Big and small flying in the air bringing me love,
Their fluttering makes me feel like they are ballet dancing,
They move from flower to flower,
They look like they are prancing, twirling and doing acrobatics.

Charlotte Caunt (7)
Burntwood J&I School, Pontefract

Butterflies

Butterflies fly high in the sky,
Up and up,
Higher and higher they fly,
Then down, down they drift,
Searching for a bed of flowers,
Fluttering, fussing,
To and fro,
Here and there,
Filling the air with their rainbow colours.

Courtney Dodd (8)
Burntwood J&I School, Pontefract

Butterfly

Butterfly, butterfly flying around a tree,
Butterfly, butterfly, let me go free,
Butterfly here, butterfly there, butterfly swirling in the air,
Butterflies red, butterflies orange, butterflies green,
And butterflies yellow,
Spotty, colourful, beautiful,
Gentle, that is the graceful butterfly.

Joseph Tolley (8)
Burntwood J&I School, Pontefract

The Butterfly Poem

Butterflies dark, butterflies bright,
Butterflies you can find in light,
Butterflies big, butterflies tiny,
Butterflies are so shiny,
Some butterflies I love,
Butterflies fly like a dove,
Butterflies are so fun,
You can find them in the sun.

Summer Tyson-Harling (7)
Burntwood J&I School, Pontefract

Butterflies

Beautiful butterflies are overwhelming at a certain height.
The butterflies flutter here and flutter there.
The butterflies can fly here and there, the more I cry the more they fly
A butterfly glides high in the sky,
Butterfly, butterfly hear me cry and sing me a lullaby.

Cody Wathey (8)
Burntwood J&I School, Pontefract

Butterflies

Under a bridge in the meadow,
The butterflies flutter by
As red as cherry, as blue as bluebells
Round and round like a graceful swan
As yellow as the sun, as black as soot
As white as a cloud.

Brown logs,
Dog running around,
Butterflies landing on flowers,
Doing that for hours,
They fly as high as towers.

Katy Cocliff (9)
Burntwood J&I School, Pontefract

Drip, Drop - Haiku

Drip, drop rain won't stop
Plip, plop in we stay all day
Drip, plop the rain stops.

Holly Philips (10)
Burntwood J&I School, Pontefract

Rain - Haiku

Drip, drop, drip, drop . . . drop,
Washes away playground fun
Plip, plop, plip, plop . . . plop.

Emma Hassall (10)
Burntwood J&I School, Pontefract

Drip, Drip, Drip - Haiku

Drip, drop rain won't stop
The rain wipes away our fun
Puddles, puddles, splash.

Samijo Cook (9)
Burntwood J&I School, Pontefract

Rain - Haiku

Plip, plop, plip, plop . . . plop
Wash away our playtime games
Cold, boring . . . inside.

Luke Hirst (10)
Burntwood J&I School, Pontefract

Sunny Playtimes - Haiku

Blue sky, birds singing
No rain today, say hooray
Children playing ball.

Whitney Harling (10)
Burntwood J&I School, Pontefract

Sunny Playtime - Haiku

Sizzle, hiss, red-hot.
Let's get started, have some fun.
Playtimes in the sun.

Rebecca Flavell (9)
Burntwood J&I School, Pontefract

Precipitation - Haiku

Drip, drop, plip, plop . . . drop
Erasing our fun and games,
Wiping fun away.

Glen Ashton (11)
Burntwood J&I School, Pontefract

Sun - Haiku

Shining down on us
Sparkling down from the blue sky
Gleaming in our eyes.

Lauren Dodd (11)
Burntwood J&I School, Pontefract

Rain - Haiku

Water bouncing down,
It is now wet everywhere,
Bored being inside.

Joseph Coe (9)
Burntwood J&I School, Pontefract

Precipitation - Haiku

Drip, drop, I hear rain,
Playground is black like the sky,
It rubs out our games.

Kimberley Lawton (10)
Burntwood J&I School, Pontefract

Rain - Haiku

Splash, splash rain won't stop
Wasting our breath of fun time
Come out Mr Sun.

Amy Tyrrell (10)
Burntwood J&I School, Pontefract

Water - Haiku

Bikini and trunks,
Pool, paddle, pool, paddle, splash,
Sun lotion and hats.

Lauren Bartrop (11)
Burntwood J&I School, Pontefract

Rain Wrestling - Haiku

Plop, plip, drip, drop . . . plop
Stair rods pounding the playground,
Pummelling our fun!

Adam Tolley (10)
Burntwood J&I School, Pontefract

Precipitation - Haiku

Look, the rain falls down
Wet people run for shelter
Umbrellas dancing.

Emma Lakin (11)
Burntwood J&I School, Pontefract

Precipitation - Haiku

Plip, plop, drip, drop . . plop
Ran lashing from heavy storms,
Wiping all our fun.

Ryan Taylor (11)
Burntwood J&I School, Pontefract

Wet Play - Haiku

Ring the bell quickly,
The rain is coming faster,
Everybody in.

Jade Chappell (10)
Burntwood J&I School, Pontefract

Rain - Haiku

Splish, splosh, splish, splosh . . . splosh
Dive in a puddle, get wet,
Go inside, dry off.

McCauley Bartrop (10)
Burntwood J&I School, Pontefract

Summer Clothes - Haiku

Sun shining brightly
Children pant, summer dresses,
T-shirts, no jumpers!

Chelsea Moss (11)
Burntwood J&I School, Pontefract

The Hot Summer - Haiku

The hot summer sun
It's too hot to go outside
The dazzling hot sun.

Marley Walker (9)
Burntwood J&I School, Pontefract

Magic Box

(Based on 'Magic Box' by Kit Wright)

I will put in my box . . .
The first scented smell of a red rose
My first sight of a fish and chip stand
A sunny beach with my sight of a lemonade stand.

I will put in my box . . .
A corner full of fresh smelling spring water,
A scrumptious bowl of mouth-watering shepherd's pie
What about literacy having sums to ten?

My box is fashioned from
Gold paper, silver paper,
Yellow paper, red paper,
And sequins.

I will keep my box
On top of my new light brown wardrobe
Surrounded by a massive green rainforest,
With my favourite flowers, *roses!*

Millie Dagless (9)
Drighlington Primary School, Bradford

The Magic Box

(Based on 'Magic Box' by Kit Wright)

I will put in that box . . .
The sight of the bright blue sea.
The sight of the bright yellow sun,
And the bright sun whistling.

I will put in that box . . .
The fresh green grass on a bright summer's day.
Shells crashing on the humongous sunny beach.
Freshly baked cheesecake with delicious creamy topping.

My box is fashioned from shiny, gleaming steel-gold.

I shall put my box under my massive bed,
Turn it into a super-charged Aston Martin.

Lewis Fox (9)
Drighlington Primary School, Bradford

Magic Box

(Based on 'Magic Box' by Kit Wright)

I will put in that box . . .
A gigantic room of delicious mouth-watering ham and cheese pizza
A massive luxury mountain of melting chocolate
The ace head banging songs of heavy metal.

I will put in the box . . .
My fave song by Green Day, 'Jesus of Suburbia'
Not any smells, but quite cold
Not very light, it's dark.

I will put in the box . . .
No feelings, it's not very boring
It's just a massive city
I'm a rock star.

My box is fashioned from gold and diamonds,
And I'll just use it
Keep it in a safe, its hinges are emeralds.

Jack Walker (9)
Drighlington Primary School, Bradford

Christmas - Cinquain

Christmas
Holly berries
Everyone having fun
Santa comes all the way through town
Xmas.

Chloë Pearce (9)
Drighlington Primary School, Bradford

The Magic Box

(Based on 'Magic Box' by Kit Wright)

I will put into that box . . .
A delicious chocolate island
A picture of my fantastic cat and dog miaowing and barking
A twitter of a new, young baby bird
A penguin playing the awesome guitar.

I will put in that box . . .
A heartwarming bark from my dog
A feel of my fuzzy, furry cat
A warm snuggle of my comfortable bed.

I will put in that box . . .
A gigantic house of mouth-watering garlic bread
A sizzling bite of a Big Mac burger yum-yum
A swishing river from the natural world.

I will put in that box . . .
A shocking swimming pool of snacks
An exciting jolly feeling
A happy thought of all around the world.

My box is fashioned from gold and rubies
With diamonds on the lid, a push up in the corner
Its hinges are made from silver and money

I shall play football on my box at the Elland Road stadium,
Then meet everybody from the Leeds team
I shall see the green grass very, very crunchy.

Jordan Sullivan (8)
Drighlington Primary School, Bradford

Rugby - Cinquain

Rugby
You will get hurt
Pass the ball to the wing
Pass the ball to five line score try!
Have fun.

Jake Carney (9)
Drighlington Primary School, Bradford

The Dragon Versus The Knight

There was a dragon
With a bad attitude
He burnt down a mine
And a school and a farmer's cornfield.

But a knight came and saved the day
He battled the dragon on a volcano
The dragon tried to eat the knight
But instead he thrashed the dragon
Who promptly flew away.

Luke Phillip West (9)
Glusburn CP School, Keighley

Four Seasons

Spring, summer, autumn and winter
Which am I?

Plants are reborn
It's back to sunny
Blackbirds to duckies,
Noses go runny.

Out of hibernation,
Relax in the breeze,
People cutting lawns, which causes a sneeze.

Jack Fletcher (10)
Glusburn CP School, Keighley

Mysterious World

In a mysterious world
There is an amazing land
And in that amazing land,
There is a big jungle.
And in that big jungle
There is a misty cave.
And in that misty cave
There is a large nest.
And in that large nest
There lay a golden egg
And from that egg
Croc came.

Ellie Bolton (10)
Glusburn CP School, Keighley

The Dragon

The dragon wakes from his slumber, his pointy ears are twitching,
For he's heard his prey right now today, and wants him in his kitchen.
His nostrils twitch, he sits up and sniffs for he has smelt a smell,
He knows that smell and likes it very well,
Human meat is nice to eat especially for snacks,
Because in his stomach he has lots of gaps.

The dragon flew through the sky, too high to be seen by you and I,
When he came down to the ground, people stopped and
                                              looked around,
For when he landed with a thump the whole world shook with a
                                              great big bump.

The dragon breathed a great big flame that would've put a volcano
                                              to shame,
Out of the fire ran a knight but he gave the dragon no big fright,
But what the dragon didn't know wouldn't help him no, no, no,
His golden scales gleamed in the light, he glared at the knight who
                                              backed off in fright,
The dragon saw his chance to move, it looked like a weird groove,
He snatched the knight in his claws and pushed him into his
                                              powerful jaws,
And then with a great big leap he jumped back home and fell asleep.

George Albone (10)
Glusburn CP School, Keighley

Golf - Haiku

I like playing golf
I smack the ball on the green
Then into the hole.

Harry Eastbury (10)
Glusburn CP School, Keighley

Seasons

Autumn
The leaves are falling off the trees,
And changing colours,
Have you seen the autumn leaves?
It's getting kind of cold.

Winter
Winter is very cold,
You can make snowmen,
And have snowball fights,
I love winter.

Spring
I'm in a land of flowers,
And watching the lambs run around,
Are you in a land of flowers?
I can't even hear a sound.

Summer
Summer is the best
You can have lots of fun
My mum thinks I'm obsessed,
You can play in the sun.

Samantha Varela (10)
Glusburn CP School, Keighley

Animals

A nimals are cool
N ever hurt a pet otherwise you're cruel
I magine you're a pet
M e and pets are also cool
A nimals, animals are so cute
L ooking at their faces, they are so neat
S troking their fur it is so sweet.

Shannon Roberts (10)
Glusburn CP School, Keighley

Wicked Poems - Haikus

Poems are quite cool
I think they are brilliant
I really like them.

Poems are the best
Poems, poems everywhere
Wicked, cool poems.

Haikus and rhyming
I will listen to them all
Poems are so cool.

Daniel Davies (10)
Glusburn CP School, Keighley

My Stupid Dog

My dog is very stupid
She lays down on her head
But even when she's quiet
She seems to make a riot.

She runs around in circles
Starting to chase her tail
She even bangs her head
When she falls over she looks dead
But really she's alive.

She's done it so many times
She stares at the doors and wonders
If I bang my head, will I be dead?

Oliver Lewis (10)
Glusburn CP School, Keighley

The Lost Elephant

An elephant strolls
Around and around,
It's escaped from the zoo
And not been found.

It's hungry and poorly
And dirty and wet
Someone needs to find it
And take it to the vet.

The poor little thing
In the dark on its own,
I can tell it needs help,
By the sound of its groan.

It's just about to fall asleep,
When it sees a bright light straight ahead,
And when he opens his eyes again,
He's back in the zoo in his nice cosy bed!

Amy Beck (11)
Glusburn CP School, Keighley

Shield - Haiku

It may defend you
It can also hurt people
It shall not shatter.

Bradley Lyle (10)
Glusburn CP School, Keighley

Season Limericks

Spring is when new flowers grow
After the cold winter's snow
Lambs running around,
Calves sit on the ground
The cold, it is starting to go.

The summer brings out the sun
Go for picnics and have a nice bun
Hikers on walks,
Friends having talks,
The children have lots of fun.

Autumn makes leaves fall to the ground,
Stepping on them makes a crunch sound.
Animals ready to hibernate
Birds starting to migrate
Hedgehogs sleeping in a leaf mound.

Winter is cold as is known
Chilling people to the bone.
Less going for a walk
Or even out for a talk
People prefer to chat on a phone.

Sam Abbey (10)
Glusburn CP School, Keighley

Dragon Day

Everyone frights and screams as he flies by
Look out he's coming, run away.
Day and night fire rises, water arrives
Look out he's coming, run away.

Benjamin Clarke (10)
Glusburn CP School, Keighley

Summer

S is for sun that shines bright
U is for unstoppable fun
M is for many friends to play with
M is for making friends on the streets
E is for excellent times with friends
R is for having real fun with your mates.

Ellis Denton (10)
Glusburn CP School, Keighley

Winter

W inter is as cold as ice
 I n your house next to the warm fire
N ew snow every minute
T oday is a new cold day
E ntertainment in the snow
R eindeer flying through the sky.

Laura Marklew (10)
Glusburn CP School, Keighley

Seasons

Spring is where all the baby animals are born
And they run around and play.
It is where all the flowers come out
Like crocuses, daffodils and lilies.
I love spring, it is a great season.

I love summer because it is when I go on holiday,
It is cool because we break up from school,
I love the sun,
It's lots of fun.

Georgia Slingsby (10)
Glusburn CP School, Keighley

My Best Friend - Haiku

My best friend is daft
He makes me and my friends laugh
He is called Daniel.

Harry Tosney (10)
Glusburn CP School, Keighley

My Sister's Hairy Left Side

She never shaves her left leg,
We've tried it with butter.
It's hairier than a tarantula,
We've tried to put her in the tub,
Spray her with the hosepipe,
My sister Hairy Left Side.

She's never had a shave,
In a million years.
She has to cover it up,
All the hair floats in the air,
Like a little butterfly.
One big blow then she goes bye-bye.
My sister Hairy Left Side.

We used the electric sander,
Just to get it off.
A few days later it grew
On the other side.
We felt scared to see it grow back.
My sister Hairy Right Side.

Ross Hall (10)
Glusburn CP School, Keighley

My Imaginary Friend

My imaginary friend
She has lots of trends,
Her name is Kim,
Her dad's name is Tim.
People laugh at me
When I hang around the tree.
Kim got ill
She had to stay still,
Two weeks later she came to me
With a medicine bill.
The price made me go up the hill
Two pounds, you're joking!

Megan Duxbury (10)
Glusburn CP School, Keighley

Fairies

How do fairies feel,
When you say they're not real,
Don't you think it makes them sad?

I believe in fairies,
Some people think I'm nuts,
I know they're there, I've seen one,
All small and glittery.

All you have to do,
Is sit and kneel,
And wait for them to come to you.

My brother says they're stupid,
My mum thinks they're great,
But no one really knows if they're real.

Megan Moore (10)
Glusburn CP School, Keighley

My Friends

I once had a friend,
Who drove me around the bend.
Her name was Mollie
And she had a big dolly,
She was eight
I tried to teach her to ice skate
And that is my friend Mollie.

And then I had a friend called Loz
But for some reason she always said 'Soz'
The last thing I remember was
Her saying soz in December
And she liked playing guns
And loved chocolate buns
And that was my friend Loz.

And now I have a friend called Ross
But when he played football he lost,
But he doesn't mind, because he is very kind,
And then we have a game of pool
Because he is very cool,
And that is my friend Ross.

Chelsey Reynoldson (10)
Glusburn CP School, Keighley

Pirates

Pirates so scary and nasty
They call other people names, pirates.

They go in the night, stealing things
That aren't theirs, pirates.

They go hunting for treasure
And when they see a little old lady
They just steal her purse, pirates.

They push people around,
They give orders to other people,
Pirates.

They wear eyepatches and wooden legs, pirates.

They go on boats and go on land
To find buried treasure, pirates.

Fergus Briggs (9)
Glusburn CP School, Keighley

Chocolate World

Every day and every night
I imagine that my dream will come true
With squishy marshmallows and yummy chocolate bars,
And other things like jelly babies,
Oh I just wish I lived in that magical world
Called Chocolate World!

With showers of chocolate
And really fun rides
And at the bottom a pool of warm melted chocolate.
For a roundabout, it is made of solid chocolate,
And the seats are chocolate bunnies
And chocolate dogs
Oh I just wish I lived in that magical world
Called Chocolate World!

Sophie Nowell (10)
Glusburn CP School, Keighley

Water

Water flows down the stream,
It makes me start to dream.
It's so cool,
This little pool,
Of water, the real thing.

The stream flows into a river,
The cold makes me quiver,
The rain starts to fall,
It makes a wall,
On top of the river.

The river crowds into the sea,
The sun makes the water flee.
Into the air,
It is still there,
That water, the real thing.

Jonathan Firth (10)
Glusburn CP School, Keighley

When School Is Over!

My sister's always with her friend,
When school is just about to end.
Mum is always on the phone,
When me and Beth get back home.
My dad is sometimes fast asleep,
As I take the quickest peek.

My mum's at work on Friday
So I go to my gran's and play.
We go to McDonald's, and have a scrumptious lunch,
Then we go home and I'm all alone.

But tomorrow is not sorrow.
Because it's the weekend, *yeah!*
We're going to have so much fun
While playing in the sun.

We'll go up to my grandma's house and never come back,
We'll sleep up there and throw a party
We'll sing and dance and never stop laughing till Monday.

Mollie Guest (9)
Glusburn CP School, Keighley

Fairies Dance

When the sun goes down and the moon comes up
The fairies in the trees will stop reading their books.
They will fly to the ground and wait for the music
Of the night to sound.
Land on the flowers and begin to dance,
They will dance all night without any fright.
And the next day they will do the same
And the same and the same.
And once again they danced all night
Without any fright.

Eleanor Ousby (10)
Glusburn CP School, Keighley

Sarah

Sarah is my special friend
With hair as black as coal.
Her eyes are blue as sky
And her teeth are white as snow.
I play with her every day
But she's not really there,
And if she suddenly did appear
It would give me a scare.
Of course, Sarah is imaginary
If you hadn't guessed,
But she's still able to get herself undressed.
She wears her hair in bunches,
Or sometimes in a plait,
Cos when she has a ponytail it always turns out slack.
That's Sarah - my friend.

Sophie Thomas (10)
Glusburn CP School, Keighley

Rain

Rain, rain, rain,
Pouring down again,
Falling on the window,
Rain, rain, rain.

Cloud, cloud, cloud,
Then it's thundering so loud
Next it's thundering no longer
Cloud, cloud, cloud.

Drop, drop, drop,
Like the sound of a dripping mop
The sun is coming out
Drop, drop, drop.

No rain, no rain, no rain,
Now I can go out again
The sun is right in sight
No rain, no rain, no rain.

Daniel Jennings (10)
Glusburn CP School, Keighley

My Sister's Pasta Hair

My sister's pasta hair is like a plate of spaghetti,
It tangles, it's slimy and it smells quite limy.

We've tried shampoo and moisturiser too,
It's just so slimy we don't know what to do.

We've tried to cut it but it just grows back,
So she gave my mum and dad a lot of backchat.

She said she hated her hair even though we knew
And pulled out a string or two.

We've been to the hairdressers, but they couldn't do anything
Even though we thought they could do many things.

So we went back home, to have a little comb.

That night we got fed up
So we just had one more look.

Alice Wild (10)
Glusburn CP School, Keighley

School

Come on, come on it's time to go
Get in the car and off to school on a Monday.
I wonder what we are doing today?
The door is open, take off your coat
Get all your things out of your drawer
It's time for morning maths.
After maths it's literacy
It is fun, fun, fun.
Shut your book and out to break
Playing on the playground running round and round.
I am out of breath now.
Ding, dong let's go in.

Come to school on a Monday, Monday, Monday
Come to school on a Monday.
I don't know why.

Lauren Boylan (10)
Glusburn CP School, Keighley

My Dog

Woof, woof, woof, goes the big black dog,
Jumping along on the chunky log,
He's only four, he's very young,
But he's already got a long, long tongue.
He's black and cuddly and is very snuggly,
He's like a warm blanket, he's called Beethoven.
He's the best pet I could ever have,
I know he loves me and I love him.
He's got a girlfriend called Neehy
Neehy Noo he always sniffs around
And always licks
He doesn't get to see her much
Sometimes he growls but I know he loves me,
Lots and lots because he's so friendly and nice
And I love him and I will forever and ever.

Adelle Edgar (9)
Glusburn CP School, Keighley

Birthday

Wow it's my birthday,
My friends have come to stay,
I've got a stripy birthday cake,
And my cousins come to play.

My sister got me a music box
That plays a quirky tune,
And my auntie got me a calendar
With a birthday circle around the 5th June.

We played musical bumps,
And ate sugar lumps,
Then we searched the garden,
When Mum did a treasure hunt.

And that was my birthday,
On the 5th June
My friends started leaving,
So I gave them a balloon,
And now I'll wait another year
Until the 5th June.

Zoe Atkinson (10)
Glusburn CP School, Keighley

Terror

Terror is dark red,
A shooting cheetah,
Smells of burning blood,
Tastes like salt,
It sounds like screaming,
Hanging out of a cheetah's mouth,
Lives in a cave.

George Strachan (9)
Lady Elizabeth Hastings CE School, Thorp Arch

Anger!

Anger is blood-red
The smell is iron burning
It tastes like a sour raspberry
The sound is like a rainforest
It feels like a crunching of an apple
It lives in a heart of a devil.

Amy Tatterton (9)
Lady Elizabeth Hastings CE School, Thorp Arch

Rose Blood Memory

Spring yellows, summer greens,
'Tis the only thing of dreams,
Winter blues, autumn reds,
And at last I lay down my head,
To sleep again a thousand years,
My pillow a haven for a million tears,
And at last my eyes do open,
It seems my heart's been given a token,
A key it seems,
A key to be a key,
A key to my lost memories
Memories of those forgotten,
Then the key recaptures my dreams,
Memory of a nightmare I kept inside,
Memory of a nightmare I tried to hide,
Then it repeats again and again,
The shivering fall, the curtain call,
A red rose I find at my feet,
At last it's beat,
Rose's black blood spills on the floor,
I close the door,
Then it's beat, what I've been defending,
I wasn't pretending,
I didn't lie nor did I cheat,
I am helped onto my feet,
A rose so gentle appears at my hand,
A river rushes past, heart's strong as stone,
And at last I'm in a world of my own . . .

Lois Saia (11)
Lady Elizabeth Hastings CE School, Thorp Arch

What's Going On?

Dear Mum,
When you were out the other day,
The dog grew wings and flew away,
The cat went out and didn't come back,
And that's when things really got bad.
A UFO came from space,
And landed by the garden gate.
It took the rabbits and the gerbil too,
And then came back for the barbeque.
And you know your favourite purple vase
It drove away in the car,
Then suddenly the guinea pigs got out of their hutch
And went round and round and round looking for their lunch,
And then your mellow yellow teapot
Mysteriously dropped,
Now if you think I'd stand for that,
You really must be mad!
So I went upstairs to see the parrot,
But he had stolen a golden carrot.
So then I decided to go to bed,
But it tried to swallow me up instead.
So when you were out the other day,
The dog got wind and blew away.
The cat went out and didn't come back,
So
I've decided instead of you,
To go to Africa for a day or two!

Lucy Binsted (10)
Lady Elizabeth Hastings CE School, Thorp Arch

My Little World

Blood-red dragons sweep and soar through purple hills and clouds,
While graceful mermaids with turquoise tails,
Swim through misty shrouds.

An emerald forest lies beside a lake
Its floor adorned with flowers,
And behind the forests, a rocky cliff
From its walls springs sparkling showers.

Silver birds with deep blue wings,
Their eyes bright and sunny,
Sing the songs of a thousand ages,
Songs as sweet as honey.

And velvety pools of moonlight
Shine where roses lie,
While stars like a million diamonds
Are scattered across the sky.

Violet butterflies with sapphire wings
Fly through blossom trees,
While sleepy nymphs lie in watery beds
Blanketed by seas.

This is the world that lies untouched
Where nothing's as it seems
The place where only I can go
This is the place of dreams.

A protection lies around it like a cherished unbroken seal,
But just because this is my little world,
It doesn't mean it's real.

Annie Hammond (11)
Lady Elizabeth Hastings CE School, Thorp Arch

My Gran's Restaurant

My Gran's restaurant
Is full of junk,
Everyone thinks it's pants.
The only decent thing about it
Is the chocolate from the shops.
There's burgers from the burger bar
And chips from the chippy,
There's hot dogs from the hot dog stall,
And,
It's all double the price!
Plus,
Gran didn't cook any of it!
So that's my Gran's restaurant . . .
Don't go there!

Emma Cook (10)
Lady Elizabeth Hastings CE School, Thorp Arch

A-Z Rules Of The New Headteacher

A lways eat really messily
B e very loud
C all people names
D on't open doors for others
E at junk food
F iddle with your bag in lessons
G et the worst mark in tests
H it other children
I gnore adults
J ump on the tables
K ick everyone
L ook out the window
M iss boring lessons
N ever listen in class
O bey naughty children
P ick your nose
Q uietly thump people
R un in the classroom
S quirt paint everywhere
T oilet roll the teachers
U nattach displays
V iolently flick pencils
W hack others
X -ray the teachers
Y odel in corridors
Z zz in tests

Guess who the new head teacher is . . .

Me!

Sophie Hannington (10)
Lady Elizabeth Hastings CE School, Thorp Arch

Happiness

Happiness is the colour of soft pink
It smells like air freshener
Happiness tastes like carbonara, the creamiest
It sounds like the laughter of a really funny joke
It feels like a fluffy blanket
Happiness lives in the brightness of the world.

Daisy Ashworth (8)
Lady Elizabeth Hastings CE School, Thorp Arch

Craziness

Craziness is the colour of bouncy blue
It smells of sausages sizzling in a pan
Craziness tastes like pancakes with sugar on top
It sounds like the craziest music you have ever heard
It feels like a banana with slimy skin
Craziness lives in the middle of your wobbly tummy
Craziness.

Joanna Barnett (10)
Lady Elizabeth Hastings CE School, Thorp Arch

My Wonderful World

Trees made of lollipops
Rivers made of chocolate
Buildings made of marshmallows
Clouds made of candyfloss.

Cars made of crisps
Roads made of rock
Rain made of Jelly Tots
Lorries made of KitKats.

Sea made of sugar
Sun made of treacle
Swimming pools made of melted toffee
Animals made of fudge.

Snow made of mints
Tornados made of liquorice
Grass made of apple laces
Mountains made of meringues
UFOs made of flying saucers
'Wake up,'
Said my teachers.

Ellie Beanland (10)
Lady Elizabeth Hastings CE School, Thorp Arch

What To Do At School

Always shout out loud
Never put your hand up in class
And don't answer any questions
Be as naughty as you can
Do not do what you're told
If you get told off just ignore them
Be very messy especially when you're having lunch and break
And especially make yourself sick on the teachers!

Stephanie Jones (10)
Lady Elizabeth Hastings CE School, Thorp Arch

What Am I?

I have spots and I run quite fast
You might see me running past.
What am I?

I have powerful legs that help me run
I hunt but I'm a main target for those hunters
What am I?

I will pounce if you come near me
I always cheat in games
I don't think you could catch me
Because I buzz like a buzzy bee!
What am I?

I have beady eyes that can see things
As fast as fleas.
What am I?

Lochlan Shaw (9)
Lady Elizabeth Hastings CE School, Thorp Arch

Why?

Daddy why is grass green?
Why do we go to school?
Why are books so readable?
Why doesn't money grow on trees?
Why is there a bedtime?
Why did veg ever get invented?
Why is Robin Gobin tallest in class?
Why can't I touch the sky?
Why does the weather change?
Why can't I get a watch like Joe Fobs?
Why is Christmas a lifetime away?
Why do you say I always ask questions?
Why do I have to do my homework?
Why isn't it my birthday now?
Why have all my Easter eggs disappeared into my tummy?
Why has the swimming pool got water in?

And

Daddy stop snoring!

Laura Dunham (10)
Lady Elizabeth Hastings CE School, Thorp Arch

The Meal

Some bacon, one egg and some garlic bread,
Some yellow rice, a drink with ice.
Pink fat ham all smothered in jam,
Next custard mixed with mustard
Now with flour lemons to make it sour,
After beans we'll do the greens

      Mummy
         I feel sick.

Francesca Harrison (10)
Lady Elizabeth Hastings CE School, Thorp Arch

The Cheetah Song

Neither fins nor flippers have I
But I spy on my food
And I have
Teeth, teeth, teeth.

Neither wings nor beak have I
But I run very fast
And I have
Teeth, teeth, teeth.

I master every movement
For I run, jump and prowl
And I flash
Teeth, teeth, teeth.

Ben McGettigan (9)
Lady Elizabeth Hastings CE School, Thorp Arch

My Fantabulous Ice Cream Sundae

This is what I like on my yummy ice cream
A scoop of cherry
A scoop of cream
A scoop of chocolate
And a scoop of ice cream
A little bit of sprinkles
A bit of strawberry wrinkles
Choc chip
Vanilla
Strawberry
A little bit of toffee
A scoop of coffee
A titchy bit of passion fruit
And for the top it has to be
The most delicious scrumptious me!

Sophie Moncaster (9)
Lady Elizabeth Hastings CE School, Thorp Arch

The Cheetah Song

Neither shell nor egg have I
But I stalk for my food
And I have
Claws, claws, claws.

Neither wings nor beak have I
But I sprint after my enemy
And I have
Claws, claws, claws.

Neither fin nor flippers have I
But I pounce powerfully and strongly
And I have
Claws, claws, claws.

I master every moment
For I sprint, pounce and stalk
And I flash
Claws, claws, claws!

Harry Stobert (9)
Lady Elizabeth Hastings CE School, Thorp Arch

If I Moved House

If I moved house I'd take:
The big weeping willow that hangs over my garage,
The view of Pool out of my window,
The birds that sing in the morning.

I wouldn't take:
The man that always shouts really loud to his dog,
The mole that makes loads of molehills,
The people that walk past shouting to each other.

I would take:
The times that I pushed my little brother in his swing,
The times that we sit on the decking and eat ice lollies.

I would not take:
The noisy cars at night racing past,
The pouring rain at night.

Selina Stoves (9)
Pool CE Primary School, Otley

If I Moved House!

If I moved house I'd take:
My best friends who live across the road
And the memories of when it snowed!

I wouldn't take:
The times when my mum burnt the food
Or the times when my brother is rude!

I'd take:
My sweet, sweet strawberry bush
And the times when we have to rush, rush, rush
But not forgetting my old hamster's grave.

I wouldn't take:
The times when my neighbours have noisy cars
Or when they are drunk.

But I'd definitely take
Waking up to the sound of tweeting.

Claudia Cohen (9)
Pool CE Primary School, Otley

If I Moved House!

If I moved house I'd take:
The sitting room where we share memories from our childhood,
The sound of trees rustling in the wind.

I wouldn't take:
The painful memories of friends and family falling ill.

I'd take:
The silence that surrounds you when you creep upstairs to bed,
The sound of laughter and shouting coming from the pub behind

the house.

I wouldn't take:
The times when I was alone or being teased.

But I would take:
All the people who mean something to me.

Evie Pedley (9)
Pool CE Primary School, Otley

If I Moved House!

If I moved house I'd take:
The time I flipped on the floor,
The sweet sound of the skylark,
The bubbles of the fish in the water feature.

I would not take:
My mad little sister
Maybe not the roof, maybe not the door.

I might take:
The barking pug next door
The time I visited Hollywood
Now that's what'd I'd take.
What would you take?

Rachael Damp (9)
Pool CE Primary School, Otley

If I Moved House!

If I moved house I'd take:
The sight of the flood coming closer and closer,
Of course I would take the view of the Chevin and the hillsides,
And I would take the sound of the robins whistling in the sun.

I wouldn't take:
The sound of my brother's steam train rattling on the floor,
And my big fat sister slouching on the couch.

I would take:
The nature of the field, like the cows, sheep and the alpacas,
And the white beautiful butterflies on the little apple tree in
the garden.

I wouldn't take:
The slimy mouths of the alpacas next to my garden.

I would take:
The view out of my bedroom window.

Beth Goldthorp (8)
Pool CE Primary School, Otley

If I Moved House!

If I moved house I'd take:
The bright green grass in the summer,
The moonlight that shines down,
The squeaky shed door!

I wouldn't take:
The cars that zoom down our road at night,
The birds that scratch on the roof.

I'd take:
The mystery stairs up to my bedroom,
The birds that sing all different ways,
Hedgehogs that crawl past.

I wouldn't take:
My next-door neighbour,
The cold floor in the conservatory.

Ellie Tempest (9)
Pool CE Primary School, Otley

If I Moved House!

If I moved house I'd take:
The hedge I kick my football against,
The drainpipe where the annoying wood pigeon lives,
The faulty floorboard,
And the wall I draw on.

I wouldn't take:
The thistles that prick me in the summer,
And the ball-snatching Ivon,
And the annoying girl next door.

I'd take:
The sound of the mice getting squished, eek!
And the cupboard door where I banged my head,
And the squeaky gate at the end of our garden.

I wouldn't take:
The dustbin truck, it wakes me up every morning
The barking dog next door,
And the annoying fox that messes up the bin.

Sam Hargreaves (9)
Pool CE Primary School, Otley

If I Moved House!

If I moved house I'd take:
My blanky which waves through the wind,
And the cat which miaows as it sings,
I would take the view which I see through the window.

If I moved house I wouldn't take:
Dot, my next-door neighbour
Because she always snores through the night.
Or Jim who drills up above me,
And I wouldn't take Mrs Clark

But I would take my toys
Which glow in the dark.

Daniel New (8)
Pool CE Primary School, Otley

If I Moved House!

If I moved house I'd take my friend's laughter.
I would take the sound of the old tree creaking.
I would not take the train tooting in the morning.
I would not take the sound of the rumble of the cars.

Bevan Rainford (9)
Pool CE Primary School, Otley

If I Moved House!

If I moved house I would take:
The robins whistling in the trees,
And the very busy, buzzy bees.

I really wouldn't take:
The next-door neighbours' Stentorian car every morning
And the timid little baby who cries every sundown.

I would take and treasure the most:
My grandma's doggie's grave.

I wouldn't take:
The dripping of the bathroom tap,
The sound of the heating coming on.

Claire Mather (9)
Pool CE Primary School, Otley

If I Moved House!

If I moved house I'd take:
Mr and Mrs Greedy the fish and their graves,
The pond with all the splashing fish
The blackbirds that sing and nest in the colourful garden outside.

I wouldn't take:
The boy next door called Sam, who is very annoying!
The loud voice of the girl up the street,
The dog that barks and barks and barks!

I'd take:
The view from the window,
The football pitch, the garden and the Chevin
Sid the ginger cat that wanders around the street.

I wouldn't take:
Edward my brother,
Screaming girls having a sleepover,
My teacher.

Rachel Barnicoat (9)
Pool CE Primary School, Otley

If I Moved House

If I moved house I'd take:
The back window because I watch my dog playing in it,
The birds' nest because of the endless songs they sing,
The big tree near the gate because we stand under it when it rains.

I wouldn't take:
My floor because it is so squeaky it hurts my ears,
My neighbours because they are very quiet it sounds horrid.

Taylor Townsend (9)
Pool CE Primary School, Otley

If I Moved House!

If I moved house I'd take:
The cows that moo in the field
The snow that I go sledging in
Sammy, Samantha and Shy my frogs in the pond.

I wouldn't take:
The view from my bedroom on a hot summer night
The music blasting out of the hot pool.

I'd take:
The Riffa Woods with the dogs and stags in
The next-door neighbour's hot pool to keep me warm
My friends for when I move school.

I wouldn't take:
The screaming children next door
The dog that barks very loud.

Hannah Liles (8)
Pool CE Primary School, Otley

If I Moved House!

If I moved house I'd take:
The nice purple colour of the walls in my bedroom
The beautiful snowdrops in our garden
And the sound of the birds singing.

I wouldn't take:
My brothers fighting against me every day
And the Wendy house door that does not shut
And it makes a noise in the night hitting the things behind it.

I'd take:
The sunny days sat on the bench in our back garden,
The wall across the road I jump off,
And I'd take the squirrel which walks along the fence
At the back of the garden.

I wouldn't take:
The patio doors that are very hard to open,
The table which always leans and knocks things over.

Jade Duncan (8)
Pool CE Primary School, Otley

If I Moved House!

If I moved house I'd take:
The sound when my cockerel goes off that wakes me
And the frog that croaks.

I would not take:
My sister telling me off
And my dad shouting at me.

I'd take:
My trampoline bouncing high
I would take all my love.

I wouldn't take:
The owls that are hooting every night
The fox that eats the chickens.

Mark Claxton-Ingham (9)
Pool CE Primary School, Otley

If I Moved House!

If I moved house I'd take:
The sound of the apple trees rustling in the wind,
My black dog that always plays with me.

I wouldn't take:
My very annoying sister because she fights with me
The cows mooing at night.

I'd take:
All the tractors and boxes.

I wouldn't take:
The cat over the road,
The long grass next door.

Jack Jefferson (9)
Pool CE Primary School, Otley

If I Moved House!

If I moved house I'd take:
My DS for fun in case I got bored
The hamster and its cage,
My bike because I've just learnt to ride.

I wouldn't take:
The fireplace,
The table and chairs,
The coat rack.

I'd take:
My TV because it's got Sky.
My shoe rack because it's fun,
My bedroom for comfort.

I wouldn't take:
My carpet,
My car,
My PlayStation.

Georgia Downes (8)
Pool CE Primary School, Otley

If I Moved House!

If I moved house I would take
The apple trees in the back garden
Because my mum makes apple crumble,
And so I can watch them grow and pick them off
Or whack them down with a stick.
My rugby ball to keep me amused there
And so I don't get bored.

I wouldn't take the howling dogs next door.
They drive me mad.

I would take the grave of my dead goldfish.

I wouldn't take my rusty climbing frame
The swing is broken it wobbles when you are on it
Because it has come loose.

Lewis Fawell (8)
Pool CE Primary School, Otley

If I Moved House

If I moved house I would take:
The old oak tree and I'd take my best blue pen ever.

I would not take:
The crows' nest or the blackbirds' nest
They're just really high in a tree.

But I would take the bunk bed
And I would take my PlayStation 2
And I would take my TV and finally my video and DVD player.

Jack Wood (8)
Pool CE Primary School, Otley

If I Moved House!

If I moved house I'd take:
The big green grass outside my house
The view of the valley from my window
And the sound of sheep in the field.

I wouldn't take:
My two brothers who are always fighting,
The squeak of the door when you walk through,
My Land Rover that rattles as you drive along.

I would take:
The noise of cars going past
The tree we climb and sit in
And my friends from school.

I wouldn't take:
The next-door neighbour's dog
The annoying girls on my street
The cold kitchen tiles.

Zak Burke (9)
Pool CE Primary School, Otley

Summertime

Summertime, summertime,
Is full of beautiful things,
Flowers in the garden and
Ice cream too, it's a wonderful
Season for me and you!

Birds are nesting up in the trees
Glistening sun up in the sky
Going on holiday, splashing
In the sea.
Come and make sandcastles
And sunbathe with me!

The sun brings out all
The flowers
Yellow, pink, red, orange, purple,
Swaying nicely in the warm
Breeze.
Bowing their heads to
The trees.

The farmer tends his crops
Of wheat, barley and rape.
The cows look after their new calfs
They're all sweet, lovely and soft.

Blossom on the trees,
Falls to the ground
Looks like white and pink confetti.
Scattered all around,
Summertime is the best
Time ever.

Rachel Hutchinson (10)
Ryhill J&I School, Wakefield

Nature Poem

The bright green grass sparkling
In the shimmering sun.
Sheep prancing about along the hillside.
Flowers swaying in the summer breeze.
Moist leaves glistening in different colours.

Charlotte Yates (9)
Ryhill J&I School, Wakefield

One Summer Evening

One summer evening, getting late
I went outside and stood by
The gate.
I lifted my head and saw a brilliant beauty,
A bird singing wonderfully and tooting.
It had a red belly with blue eyes, it woke
Me up and gave me a warm feeling
Inside.

What it did was make me
Survive because I really wanted to shut my eyes,
But all it did was perch on me and sang me a song which
Reminded me of nature.
But I decided all I could do was enjoy the evening and sing along
Too.

Annie Burgess (9)
Ryhill J&I School, Wakefield

Nature Is In The Air

N ature is all around us,
A nimals are grazing happily,
T he birds are nesting in the trees,
U nderneath lays a deer in the cool summer air,
R ain is helping the flowers grow,
E very day more nature comes.

Jennifer Cliff (10)
Ryhill J&I School, Wakefield

Spring Is In The Air

Spring has begun when the first flowers push their shoots
Out of the soil,
Blossom surrounds trees like fluffy clouds.
Spring green leaves sprouted out from every angle,
Birds feed the young and collect twigs to make a new home,
Bluebells shoot out of the ground,
Bright yellow sunflowers stretch out in the sun.

Charlie Schofield (9)
Ryhill J&I School, Wakefield

The Mist On The Lake

The mist drifts on
The lake as it ripples
Side by side, the crumbly
Mountains block the way
Of the candyfloss clouds,
A pack of branches rustle
Over the cobwebbed house.
Emerald trees surround the
Camouflaged cottage
The mist gathers the
Smell of damp earth
Filling the cracked.
An ancient boat
Lies rocking against the
Banking as the wind starts to
Blow and the sky gets darker
The mist stands still, the
Lake freezing, a gust of wind
Swirls away the smell of damp and
Wet, the trees of brown like soldiers
On the green grass the shimmering
Lake, lifting the boat, bobbing up and
Down like a chocolate box picture,
Frozen in time.

Tiffany Mallinder (10)
Ryhill J&I School, Wakefield

Nature Poem

Grass is as green as the trees.
Sky is as blue as the sea.
Clouds, as fluffy as candyfloss
Floating along the mountaintops.
Trees swaying from side to side.
Animals hunting for food.

Kelsey Maguire (10)
Ryhill J&I School, Wakefield

My Funny Friends

Charlotte's into music
Her favourite band's Green Day!
Sara thinks that she's a horse
And goes round saying neigh!

Freddie's into rock and roll
He loves heavy metal.
Chrissie moved to this school
And has found it hard to settle!

Rosie's into fashion
She loves cool, new shoes!
Emma's really rich and she'll soon be on a cruise!

Macca loves fighting
He pretends to be a ninja!
Beccy loves her silky hair
And is proud to be a ginger!

Danny's into running
He loves doing races!
Everyone is different
Different smiles, different names, different faces!

Bethany Quinn (11)
St Joseph's RC Primary School, Wetherby

Hazza And Pozza

Pozza is lazy,
Hazza is crazy,
Barking all day long,
Although, they know it's wrong!

Hazza and Pozza scratch and go mad,
Watching me write in my diary pad,
Hazza and Pozza have nice groomed hair,
They also watch me and stare!

Hazza and Pozza feel like they're part of your heart,
Zooming around in a cart.
Hazza and Pozza sit in their box,
Barking at a fox.

Pozza plays cute,
And sits on a boot,
Hazza jumps around,
And plays on the ground.

Hazza follows me around the house,
And he never runs after a mouse,
Pozza hardly moves from her basket,
And she hates the ping of elastic!

Pozza is lazy,
Hazza is crazy,
Barking all day long,
Although they know it's wrong.

Katy Hewison (10)
St Joseph's RC Primary School, Wetherby

School Days

Monday was as dull and boring as ever.
We got spelling, the hardest word was feather.
I have got a lot of practising to do,
I have got maths homework too.

Tuesday was a bit better than Monday
We had PE with Mr Tay.
Terry is the best at ball,
None can throw to me I am too tall.

Wednesday was quite fun
At playtime we had a great time in the sun
My teacher gave me a gold star
At home time my mum picked me up in her new car.

Thursday was really great
But I did fall out with my best mate
Our class did music in the afternoon
Me and Ian made up a really good tune.

Friday was super cool
We went on our school trip to the swimming pool.
We got extra play
We had great fun that day.

My week started off not so first class
But we did do fun maths
I was told off a few times
But during the week I was not forced to do lines!

Georgia Staniforth (11)
St Joseph's RC Primary School, Wetherby

Seasons

Winter is the colour blue,
Icy and cold
The snow, fresh and new
Too cold to hold.

Spring brings love,
Birds are singing
I can hear a dove
And the church bells ringing.

Summer sounds like ice cream vans
Exciting colours now
People getting tans
And everyone is going, 'Wow!'

Autumn reminds me of ginger,
No leaves on the trees,
Little kids running around,
Pretending to be ninjas.

The four seasons are these.

Gemma Westoby (10)
St Joseph's RC Primary School, Wetherby

My Brother

My brother is silly,
And he's really fun.
He likes nothing better
Than a sticky toffee bun.

Pasta is his favourite food,
He's the fastest eater in his school.
He loves cheese on his food
But it depends on his mood!

His favourite colour is still blue,
That's probably why he has a blue kazoo.
He even has his own blue loo!
Plus his train that goes choo choo.

He likes to play on the PlayStation a lot,
His funniest game is about a robot
He never lets me on it,
But hey so what!

Matthew Milligan (10)
St Joseph's RC Primary School, Wetherby

In The Headmistress' Office

Oh dear, I'm gonna be sick
It's all because of that boy called Mick!
He got me into trouble today,
I don't know what the headmistress will say.

Now I really think I'm doomed
At least that's what all my friends assumed.
I really didn't do anything
Well, I did force Laura to sing.

I did trip Jo up in the hall
And then I lost Gemma's bouncy ball!
I didn't do much, just a few pranks
Then my friend turned me in and I said, thanks.

It was Mick that turned me in
He's just committed a great big sin!
I can't believe that he was my friend,
He's really driving me round the bend.

The headmistress is on her way
Oh dear, oh no what shall I say?
I've made up my mind I'm gonna lie
But she could find out and then I'll die!

The headmistress is here
Now I have to face my biggest fear
She grabbed me by the collar and said,
'You stupid girl,' so I hit her on the head!

She was gobsmacked at what I did
I told her I was only a kid.
She said that she would 'call my folks'
I said, 'Come on, I only did a few jokes!'

Suddenly she changed into a shade of green,
And turned into a killing machine.
She gobbled me up, so here I am,
Stuck in her tummy with a piece of lamb!

The moral of this poem is don't be cheeky,
To your headmistress!

Antonia Ward (10)
St Joseph's RC Primary School, Wetherby

My New Car

Sitting in the garage is a car
That I nicked from a superstar.
It's fast and cool,
I can even drive it to school.

The car is a Ford
I treat it like a lord.
The wheels are gold
But not that bold!

My old car is at the dump
With the other lump.
I take my new car out at night
And it gleams in the light.

Now there's a new Ford out
If I don't get it I'll shout.
So look out everyone,
I want a new car,
And if I don't get it,
I'll nick another one from a superstar!

Daniel Dean (11)
St Joseph's RC Primary School, Wetherby

Autumn

Autumn is a time for family walks
Through a dark wood with hawks
Flying among the branches,
Looking for prey on the dark woody floor.

It smells like decaying leaves
Heaves and heaves of leaves all crunchy
All in great big piles
On this autumn day.

It tastes like ripe juicy apples,
For a big grey dapple horse.
As a romantic couple ride down the lane,
To get married and breathe the sweet air.

The sound is a crunch
As you step on the leaves on the ground
As you spin around and around,
On your evening walk in the dark woods
With the hawks flying above your head.

Sarah Murtha (11)
St Joseph's RC Primary School, Wetherby

The Stupid Fool!

Today at 3.00
At our school
A robber broke in
The stupid fool!

He wrecked all our books
And even the pens
And after that,
He broke into the men's.

The police arrived,
It was rather dim,
The head teacher is cross,
And all is looking grim.

Everything is broken
We'll have to order more
A riot is breaking out
My ears are getting sore!

Much later that morning
Back at our place
Everything is broken,
It's a big disgrace!

Detectives came round
Snooping for clues
Everyone is silent
And full of the blues.

The teacher's looking angry
The teacher's looking cross
What are we going to do?
We've had a terrible loss!

Today at 3.00
At our school
A robber broke in
The stupid fool!

Katie Lambert (10)
St Joseph's RC Primary School, Wetherby

Why Me?

Sitting in a pet shop all day long,
Listening to the canary in full song!
Sitting in the pet shop all day
No company - just some hay!

People staring into my cage,
It feels like I've been here for an age.
I wonder why it had to be me
Why couldn't I be free?

Wishing I could be in the wild,
Instead, I'm here, getting picked up by a small child.
I wish that I could run away,
Instead I stay here - yet another day

Been in captivity my whole life long,
Listening to the canary in full song!
Sitting in the pet shop all day,
Been here all my life and here I will stay!

Rebecca Lees (11)
St Joseph's RC Primary School, Wetherby

The World Cup!

People piling in
Trying to buy tickets
People will be cheering for goals
Not for the wickets!

        You can see all the colours now
        Of all the different teams
        It's like the colours of the rainbow,
        Ready all to beam.

All the fans are roaring
Cheering on their team!
Hoping that they'll win
Looking very keen.

        It's stinking really bad
        Of cigarettes and beer
        That's the worst thing
        With shouting in my ear!

I can feel the atmosphere now,
It's the best feeling in the world.
Here comes the Mexican Wave,
With a little twirl.

        Here comes Cole,
        Running down the wing,
        If he scored a goal,
        He would be a king!

Now here comes a chance
It's for Paul Scholes
Can he score it!
It's a goal, it's a goal!

        The World Cup is ours,
        It's finally won!
        It took 40 years
        And the job is done!

John Tehrani (11)
St Joseph's RC Primary School, Wetherby

A Normal School Day!

Hannah's hitting,
Rachel's rushing
Kaylum's kicking
Patrick's pushing.

James is jibbering,
Tina's talking,
Sarah's screaming,
Wilson's walking.

Wilber's washing,
Debra's dressing,
Timothy's tying,
Maria's messing.

Flossie's fussing,
Lia's lining,
Rebecca's reading,
Wendy's whining.

Oliver's opening,
Michael's munching,
Eve's eating,
Linda's lunching.

Laura's leaning,
Mr Man's miming,
Sindy's swimming,
Tamsen's timing.

Winifred's waving,
Helen's hunching,
Max's meeting,
Peter's punching.

Tracey
    Trips
        End of day!

Danielle Bowdler (11)
St Joseph's RC Primary School, Wetherby

My Auntie Sue

My auntie Sue is really cool
But sometimes she might act like a fool.
She loves to play games and call people names.
She loves to have fun and eat a cream bun.

My auntie Sue takes me to the shops
She always wants to buy me lollipops.
She buys loads of clothes and makes lots of jokes,
She buys herself sweets and me lots of treats.

My auntie Sue looks her best
Never ever does she look a mess.
She's busy all the time, she's really kind.
She comforts me when I'm feeling blue and
That is my auntie Sue!

Rebecca Crooks (11)
St Joseph's RC Primary School, Wetherby

Pip And Suzie

My cats are very sweet,
Waiting for their food.
But cannot wait to eat their raw, tasty meat,
Now they will be happy, in a good mood.

My cats are very good fighters,
They aren't afraid to get hurt.
Surprisingly they don't bite,
Unlike the dog called Burt.

Once my cats were naughty,
They brought a bird in the house.
And when my dad was forty,
They decided to bring in a mouse.

When food is around,
Pip and Suzie hover,
They sit and beg on the ground,
Sometimes though - they are a bother.

James Lewington (11)
St Joseph's RC Primary School, Wetherby

My Aunt Sally

The first thing you'll notice about my aunt Sally is
That the first thing you'll hear her say is tar to her family!
Tar to her friends, tar to the cat, tar to the neighbours in the wooden
old flat.

The second thing you'll notice about my aunt Sally is
She loves to dance with her friends and family.
She hates to dance by herself,
But with a little company, you'll see her normal self.

The third thing you'll notice about my aunt Sally is
She's always up for a laugh with my great aunt Tally,
She never laughs when she's on her own,
But that's why she always moans.

The last thing you'll notice about my aunt Sally is
Her clothes, errgh, you don't want to know.
That frilly pink dress with the green, spotty bow,
That's my aunt Sally.

Rebecca Burrows (11)
St Joseph's RC Primary School, Wetherby

Fear

Fear is as blue as the shocking lightning
It sounds like a swimming pool getting smaller and tightening.
The taste is as bitter as the salty sea,
It gives me shivers down to the knee.
Fear reminds me of a great big drop,
Me falling into a candy shop
It reminds me of a bit of lightning,
I don't want to think about it because it's frightening.

Fear has come, fear has gone,
Now I don't have to smell that pong
Fear I really have beat,
Now I can have a seat and rest my feet.
Then I woke up,
On the floor was a spilt cup.
When fear had gone it was a dream,
And now all I can see is cream, cream, cream.
Then the cream had gone,
Now I had to smell that horrid pong.
I had fear out of my mind,
So I watched TV to try and unwind.
I have won the battle - fear has gone,
I am the best - number one.

Oliver Boyes (10)
St Joseph's RC Primary School, Wetherby

The Playground

The boys are playing football
The girls are playing netball
People are shouting,
People are rapping.

Girls are screaming high in their voice
They are also squealing!
Boys are dashing all around
Girls are bashing a ball on the ground.

Boys are doing pranks
Girls are doing a dance
The boys are playing basketball
The girls are playing baseball.

Dominic Bateman (10)
St Joseph's RC Primary School, Wetherby

Summer

Summer is a season which is very, very hot,
And everyone around you is playing about a lot.
Summer has a mix of bright colours,
Like orange, red and yellow,
As I sit under the sun,
Eating marshmallows.

Summer feels hot on my skin,
It makes me have a huge big grin!
Summer might sometimes be a bit too hot,
But so what?

Anna Bateman (10)
St Joseph's RC Primary School, Wetherby

Footy Man

Hey, yo my name is Joe
Here's my rap and away we go!

I was born in Leeds, 1994
The next I remember was seeing Leeds score!

Kelly, Kewell and all the rest,
Leeds United are the best!

So I trained on up and got really good,
I went on down to a footy neighbourhood!

I'm on fire I think the team's fly
Then I hurt my leg - in the blink of an eye!

The worst thing is I got scouted for Leeds
I was sitting at home praying for a miracle please!

I healed up quick,
And my skills were cool and slick!

But then I broke my arm falling from a stool,
Then I spoke to my coaches and they said, 'Not cool!'

I got dropped from the squad cos of my injury
And that's one thing that really depressed me!

I had recovered I wondered where to go,
And my friend said, 'Come with us, it's bo!'

I went on down they were pretty good,
We won the cup, so I left the neighbourhood!

Next stop Manor Park,
Their coach Dave had a bit of a bark!

They were skilful and mean,
They worked like a well oiled machine!

I had to go,
And that was not bo.

I heard about Collingham they were not so far
They were only training in Boston Spa!

I went on back,
I knew I couldn't slack!

There weren't many spaces,
So I had to put a smile on the coaches' faces!

So here we are, here I am
Back playing for Collingham.

That was my story,
I hope I didn't bore ye

Just one more thing,
May 21st, Leeds are gonna win!

Joseph McGolpin (11)
St Joseph's RC Primary School, Wetherby

Ready, Steady, Go

Driving to the Olympic Games
Ready, steady, go.
Cannot wait for all the fame
Ready, steady, go.

As we all go through the gates
Ready, steady, go.
Jumping for joy with my mates
Ready, steady, go.

As we watch the runners run past
Ready, steady, go.
As the flag is pulled up the mast
Ready, steady, go.

News just in that I just heard
Ready, steady, go.
Colin Jackson has come third
Ready, steady, go.

As they finish round the track
Ready, steady, go.
Now we have to set off back
Ready, steady, go.

Dominic Stubbs (10)
St Joseph's RC Primary School, Wetherby

In My Own World

All I wanted was a little attention
But all I got was detention.
As the bell rang,
I went to the most boring room ever
Alone with Mr Trevor.
I started to think of my own world,
No trouble ever, no Mr Trevor!
All bubbles float in the world -
The floor yellow-covered with marshmallow, chocolate houses.
Liquorice drops and lollipops!
Coming down from the sky,
Popadom boats, rivers that are fizzy,
Sand sherbet like sand all sweet and sugary!
My special own land -
Just for me, life would be so grand!
There went the bell, time for home,
Dream all night when I'm alone!

Laura Hughes (11)
St Joseph's RC Primary School, Wetherby

My Fantastic Fun-Filled Holiday

Holidays are for quality time,
With you, me and Dad with the wine.
Holidays are really fun,
So everyone can stop and enjoy the sun.

Blue is the colour of the beautiful sea,
Then a horrible bee came and stung me.
When I'm on holiday I feel free,
Sometimes I need shelter under a tree.

It's now time to have a barbeque,
I think it will be meat for you.
We played in our inflatable boat,
The problem was, it wouldn't float!

I went to get some ice cream from the shop,
But I saw a lovely-looking lollipop.
Remember everybody, have fun,
On your super holiday in the sun.

Amy Goodby (11)
St Joseph's RC Primary School, Wetherby

This Is Just To Say

I have scratched
The game you
Brought me which
You probably wanted to play.

I was very bad to
Scratch the game
But it is done now
I am sorry.

It is too late to go
Back to the shops
Now they are closed
Down now, too late.

It was very fun
To play, I enjoyed
Playing I wish I
Could play it now.

Forgive me for what I did
What I have done
It was too childish for
You anyway.

Why did it happen?

Dion Phillips (11)
St William's RC Primary School, Bradford

The Haunted House

Dark, mysterious and gloomy,
The massive mansion stood;
Silhouetted in the moonlight -
Glaring down upon a wood.

I pressed on through the darkness,
Drawing closer to the derelict dwelling;
When suddenly from the house came
The sound of someone yelling.

The shrilly sound pierced my ears,
I sweat and shook with fright,
But deciding something had to be done -
I set off up into the night.

And then upon an impulse,
I shoved against the door,
Only to find it caved in -
Into a heap upon the floor.

The mansion was quite desolate,
Cobwebs draped everywhere;
Moonlight trickled in through a window,
And I smelt mould in the air.

The hairs on my neck stood on end,
As I ventured down the hall;
Inspecting the corroded shelves -
And the rapidly rotting wall.

The door at the end of the passageway,
Swung inwards with a creak;
To reveal a sinister skeleton -
Who let out a hollow shriek.

He grasped me in one bony hand,
And dragged me to the door;
I squirmed out of his steely grip -
And dashed across the floor.

Hannah Weston (11)
St William's RC Primary School, Bradford

Who Am I?

The person who knew me
And I never knew,
The person I knew
But never knew too.

> The person who watches
> Me when I sledge
> The person who loves me
> When I'm on the edge.

The person who guards
Me when I'm slow
The person who someday
I will know.

> The person who cares
> For me when I'm ill
> The person who never
> Foots the bill.

The person I love
Day and night
This person I love
Like my lost kite.

Selina Roberts (11)
St William's RC Primary School, Bradford

The Haunted House

Dark, mysterious and gloomy,
The massive mansion stood,
Dark and derelict, the mansion towered,
A haunted vision I saw.

Dark, mysterious and gloomy
I stepped up to the door,
As it opened creaking
The creepy mansion revealed
Shambles inside, shambles outside,
Why did I come in?

I walked further into the house,
Until I came to a door,
Red, rusty, faded paint,
How distressing it looked.

As I opened the rusty door
It revealed a nasty surprise,
Skeletons, dead bodies,
Blood dripping like mad,
Derelict, distressing
What a horrific surprise.

Ethan Asante (11)
St William's RC Primary School, Bradford

The Haunted House

Dark, mysterious and gloomy
The massive mansion stood
It covered a lot of space, it was quite roomy,
I didn't know if I should.

Tentatively I pushed open the door
I stepped on the blood-soaked floorboards.
I heard a shriek and saw a pattern of blood across the floor
Suddenly I lost my vocal chords.

Eloping up the stairs
I saw a barricaded door
Then I thought, *who cares?*
But when I entered the room I wasn't sure.

To my horrific terror I saw a great skeleton
I nearly collapsed in a heap
I wished I hadn't skipped in detention
Bravely I made a dashing leap.

My heart pumping rapidly,
I sprinted down the stairs
I shattered the door violently
I knew I'd have nightmares.

Frantically I ran
I ran till got to my house
In my frantic surge I knocked an old man
I opened the door and slipped onto the couch.

Adil Malik (11)
St William's RC Primary School, Bradford

This Is Just To Say

I have eaten
The buns
That were on
The side

And which
You were probably
Saving
For the party.

Forgive me
They were luscious
So tempting and
So chocolatey.

Alexandra (11)
St William's RC Primary School, Bradford

My Teacher Is A Monster

My teacher is a monster
Who screams and shouts all day,
And if you are naughty,
She will make you pay!

My teacher is a monster,
Who wears ripped up clothes,
Her fingers are bony
And as long as half a hose!

My teacher is a monster
Who hangs cobwebs round the room,
If you don't put your hand up,
Your life will turn to doom!

My teacher is a monster
Who eats children in May.
She lives in the forest,
And likes to sleep on hay!

My teacher is a monster
Who talks with a hiss,
And I really, really hope,
She doesn't read this.

Elanor Murray (10)
St William's RC Primary School, Bradford

The Haunted House

Dark, mysterious and gloomy
The massive mansion stood.
Walking to the haunted house,
Though the top was dripping blood!
Holding onto the door handle
I knew that I could.

The door flew open
I walked slowly into the house
And I suspected that I had
Seen a ghost!
Or was it flying toast?

I ran up the stairs till I came to the top!
And then found monstrous gallons of pop.
I walked into the master bedroom,
There in the corner was a huge mop!

I came out of the master bedroom
I saw in my arm a knife
I tried to take it out
This could be the end of my life!

I thought it was a dream
And there I was in my bed,
Fast asleep screaming in my head
My head, my head!

Macauley Spivey (10)
St William's RC Primary School, Bradford

The Flying Horse

Galloping, galloping over the fields,
Its solid black coat shining.
Her hooves are thudding,
Against the freshly cut grass.
What do I see?
It's a horse.
I jump on her back and feel her silky mane,
It is as soft as a cushion.
Then, I rise up high in the sky.
We jump over the clouds,
I feel as if am in Heaven.

Leah Ward (10)
Sharlston Community School, Wakefield

The Open Door

(Based on 'The Door' by Miroslav Holub)

Go and open the door,
Maybe outside there is
A beautiful white horse,
Galloping around the
Grassy field,
Its silvery mane blowing
In the wind.

Maybe there is a cute
Little mouse,
Nibbling on some cheese
In the field.

Maybe there are some scissors,
Cutting the grass for you,
In the morning daylight.

Maybe there is a rainbow,
Making its way across the sky,
With lots of different colours.

Hollie Joyce (9)
Wakefield Girls' High School, Wakefield

If I Weren't Me

If I were an animal I would be a
Charming chimpanzee,
Swinging swiftly on an old cocoa tree.

If I were a bird I would be a
Peacock,
Walking proudly with my feathers out.

If I were a piece of furniture I would be a
Comfy squashy sofa,
As soft as silk relaxing in the shade.

If I were a musical instrument I would be a
Violin,
Waiting to have my delicate strings touched
By the bow made of silk horse hair.

If you could eat me I would be a
Piece of melting milk chocolate,
That would make your throat fizz and bubble.

If I were a vehicle I would be a
Quad bike,
Zooming faster than a horse's gallop along a golden track.

If I were a weather I would be the
Arrogant wind,
Whistling away and flying over oceans and deserts.

If I were a famous person I would be
Sharon Osbourne, waiting for Louis
To say something terribly rude and to pour ice-cold water over his
head.

But I like being me because
I can talk and enjoy playing
With my friend.

Lucy Booth (9)
Wakefield Girls' High School, Wakefield

If I Weren't Me

If I were an animal I would be a
Palomino horse trotting gracefully
Through the beautiful fields.

If I were a bird I would be a,
Red-breasted robin
Singing in the sunlit sky.

If I were a piece of furniture I would be a
Soft comfy green armchair
In a beautiful light
Living room.

If you could eat me I would be a
White bar of chocolate melting in the
Glistening sun.

If I were a musical instrument I would be a
Beautiful brown guitar, with someone tickling my strings
And playing a soft melody.

If I were a vehicle I would be a
Silver Jaguar going to Hollywood speeding
Along the straight
Clear highway.

If I were a famous person I would be
Zara Phillips
A famous 3 day eventor.

If I were the weather I would be the
Rain, making plants grow and making spiderwebs
Sparkle in the sunlight.

But I like being me because I like my family,
Especially my sister, my mum and my dad.

Amber Balmforth (8)
Wakefield Girls' High School, Wakefield

If I Weren't Me

If I were an animal I would be a silver dolphin,
So I could splash gracefully in the glistening blue sea.

If I were a piece of furniture I would be a king-sized, comfortable bed
With four posters and a large
Turquoise duvet waiting patiently for someone to snuggle up on me.

If you could eat me I would be a tasty toffee pudding with caramel
sauce trickling down me and a soft layer of melted chocolate at the
top.

If I were a musical instrument I would be an enormous drum kit
So I could wake up my parents
Early in the morning when the sun is rising. *Bang!*

If I were a bird, I would be a tiny bluebird
Cheeping cheerfully, waiting happily for my mother to feed me
delicious food.

If I were a vehicle I would be a large red truck
Decorated with colourful flowers.

If I were the weather, I would be the hot summer so I could keep
everyone warm and come out so that everyone else can come out and
play.

If I were a famous person I would be a mega movie star so that I could
earn a fortune and buy a massive mansion.

But I like being me because it's fun and I go to a brilliant school
And have brilliant parents.

Disha Shetty (9)
Wakefield Girls' High School, Wakefield

If I Weren't Me

If I were an animal I would be a
Baby deer with snowflake spots
Exploring bravely in the woods.

If I were a bird I would be a
Toucan looking at the beautiful rainforest.

If I were a piece of furniture I would be a door
To keep everybody out of darkness.

If you could eat me I would be
Ice cream, cold and strawberry flavoured.

If I were a musical instrument I would be a
Harp playing quickly and quietly all day long.

If I were a vehicle I would be a
Plane gliding gracefully over England.

But I like being me because
I have all my friends
And family to comfort me.

Siobhan McGrath (8)
Wakefield Girls' High School, Wakefield

If I Weren't Me

If I were a musical instrument I would be a
French horn glittering in the sun
Whilst being played.

If I were a vehicle I would be a
Motorbike with my red seat
Glittering in the sun.

If I were an animal I would be
An American golden long-haired
Cocker spaniel snoring loudly
In my bed.

If I were a bird I would be
A golden eagle with my feathers
Spread out whilst gliding.

If you could eat me I would be
A chocolate, melting in the sun.

If I were a piece of furniture
I would be a chaise longue lying
Lazily in the sunlight.

But I like being me because
My mum and dad love me.

Jessica Baker-Hollinworth (9)
Wakefield Girls' High School, Wakefield

If I Weren't Me

If I were a vehicle I would be a
Black, gleaming limousine to take,
Famous popstars everywhere.

If I were an animal I would be a
Black-spotted jaguar pouncing quickly,
Through the tropical jungle.

If I were a bird I would be a
Tiny blue tit sitting on a wooden bird table,
Waiting to be fed.

If I were a musical instrument I would be a
Silver flute playing softly through the night.

If I were a piece of furniture I would be a
Big wooden clock ringing loudly
Through the tall house.

If you could eat me I would be a
Deep red seeded strawberry
Nestling cosily on a light green twig.

If I were the weather I would be
White cold snow so people could
Go through me on pink flowered skis.

If I were a famous person I would be
Princess Charlotte to sit in a golden carriage
Going through a screaming crowd of people.

But I like being me because of
All the fun things that I do,
Like horse riding.

Charlotte Maule (9)
Wakefield Girls' High School, Wakefield

If I Weren't Me

If I were a bird I would be a
Big male peacock
Shimmering my beautiful deep coloured tail
As I wait for
A mate.

If I were an animal I would be a
Coco chocolate Labrador
Chasing my tail wildly
As I play.

If I were a musical instrument I would be a
Long glistening silver flute
Waiting to be played.

If I were a piece of furniture
I would be a
Big comfortable black chair
Sitting in front of a widescreen TV
With a warm fire by my side.

If I were the weather I would be
Snow
Gently drifting softly to the ground.

If I were a famous person I would be
Britney Spears
Singing 'Just a little bit more'.

If you could eat me I would be a
Long, dark chocolate bar
Wanting to be snapped.

But I like being me because
I have family
And friends.

Rosalind Hunter (9)
Wakefield Girls' High School, Wakefield

If I Weren't Me

If I were a bird I would be a chubby blue tit with floating wings
Smoothly dancing round in circles
Proud of my lemon, yellow, fluffy chest.

If I were a piece of furniture,
I would be a creamy leather pouffe, with a
Velvet cloth top.

If I were an animal, I would be a fluffy,
Cuddly and patchy guinea pig
Who moves joyfully through the feather-light sawdust,
Gently moving my soft paws.

If I were a musical instrument, I would be a violin,
Painted in a purple, smooth, sparkly coating with strings
Strumming from the resin bow.

If you could eat me, I would be a pot of gold, sticky
Honey, dripping onto the buttery toast.

If I were a vehicle I would be a motorbike with loud aggressive noises
Vibrating through the ground,
With silver handles gleaming like a magnificent beast
In the light of the white mighty moon.

If I were weather I would be a golden ball of hot fire
Which burns the ground with light.

If I were a famous person,
I would be Hilary Duff with long wavy blonde hair
And glittering eyes from the disco ball.

But I like being me because it's fun and exciting
Although I would love to fly and I like having friends
With lovely personalities.

Stephanie Cheetham (9)
Wakefield Girls' High School, Wakefield

Open The Door

(Based on 'The Door' by Miroslav Holub)

Go and open the door
Maybe outside there's
A genie in a magic lamp,
Surrounded by magic jewels,
With a puff of smoke
Coming out of it hastily.

Maybe there is a
Pterodactyl swishing its tail at me
And giving me a ride on its back.

Maybe there is a
World map
Taking me wherever
I want to go.

Maybe there is
A gust
Of wind
Cleaning up
The leaves in the garden
So I do not have to do
My chores
Yippee!

Jessica Johnston (9)
Wakefield Girls' High School, Wakefield

The Open Door

(Based on 'The Door' by Miroslav Holub)

Go and open the door
Maybe outside there's
A horse riding into the sunset
With a beautiful mane flowing out
Behind him.

Maybe there's
An exotic Caribbean island
With a bright blue sea where dolphins
Leap with joy.

Maybe there are
Trees singing happily together
With their silver leaves drifting
Gently to the ground.

Maybe there are
Giant mountains with the sun
Glistening on the snow-peak tops.
Where skiers battle for the championship.

Georgia Houston (9)
Wakefield Girls' High School, Wakefield

The Open Door

(Based on 'The Door' by Miroslav Holub)

Go and open the door
Maybe outside there's
Trees with golden leaves
Shimmering in the sun.

Maybe there are
Fairies in the midnight blue
Making plants grow.

Maybe there is a black slinky cat
Walking along the road.

Maybe there are
Apples dropping from blossom trees
Glistening and sparkling as they fall.

Philippa Lister (8)
Wakefield Girls' High School, Wakefield

The Open Door

(Based on 'The Door' by Miroslav Holub)

Go open the door
Maybe outside there's
A snowstorm fiercely
Throwing snow around.

Maybe there is
A magical land
When each day is Christmas
Or snow deep
Enough to reach
Your knees.

Maybe there are
Two people walking
On their ancient wooden hands
With baggy clothes on.

Maybe there are
Stars twinkling in
The dazzling night sky.

Emily Mappin (8)
Wakefield Girls' High School, Wakefield

The Open Door

(Based on 'The Door' by Miroslav Holub)

Go and open the door
Maybe there's
A Palomino horse waiting for
You to ride it.

Maybe there is
A soft golden puppy
Outside on your doorstep
Waiting for you to feed it.

Maybe there is
£1000 waiting for
You to spend it.

Maybe there is
The biggest bar of
Chocolate waiting for
You to eat it.

Kristina Hall-Jackson (9)
Wakefield Girls' High School, Wakefield

The Open Door

(Based on 'The Door' by Miroslav Holub)

Go and open the door,
Maybe outside there's
A fairy jumping in the garden
Making chocolate flowers grow.

Maybe there are
Some golden leaves playing tricks
On the sparkling, silver moon.

Maybe there is
A big birthday cake
Singing happy birthday to you.

Maybe there are
Some trees walking in
The glittering snow.

Rimanee Kaur (8)
Wakefield Girls' High School, Wakefield

The Open Door

(Based on 'The Door' by Miroslav Holub)

Go and open the door
Maybe outside there's a mirror fish,
Swimming smoothly in the sparkling blue sea
Swishing its little tail and flapping its silver fins.

Maybe there are basketballs,
Scattering rapidly around the dusty floor,
Bouncing as high as they can.

Maybe there's a bluebird,
Swooping swiftly in the sky
Tweeting a tuneful song.

Maybe there are bottlenosed dolphins
Dancing in the dazzling sea,
Going off into the sunset.

Emily Peace (9)
Wakefield Girls' High School, Wakefield

The Open Door

(Based on 'The Door' by Miroslav Holub)

Maybe outside there's a
Golden ball for me and you to
Play with.

Maybe there is a pony pacing
The street at midnight.

Maybe there is a talking
Rabbit to keep me company.

Maybe there is a fairy to
Grant my wishes.

Costandia Demetriou (9)
Wakefield Girls' High School, Wakefield

The Open Door

(Based on 'The Door' by Miroslav Holub)

Go and open the door,
Maybe there's a
Magic tree whistling in the breeze
Or a room which is calling your name
Through the blank walls.

Maybe there are fish,
Shimmering in the Arctic icy pond
Or an iron steaming to itself,
In the cold damp room.

Maybe there's a book
On a lonely empty shelf,
Waiting to be read,
Or a pencil with a point so sharp and fragile,
No one dares touch it.

Maybe there is a pack of cards,
With kings, queens and jokers beautifully
Drawn, laughing and joking to themselves,
Or a world with nature so beautiful
But waiting to be cared for.

Holly Clifton (9)
Wakefield Girls' High School, Wakefield

The Open Door

(Based on 'The Door' by Miroslav Holub)

Go and open the door,
Maybe outside there's
A talking car with
Mysterious eyes blinking.

Maybe there is
A red Chinese dragon
Dancing on the street.

Maybe there is
A magic garden
With blue genies
Doing magic tricks.

Maybe there are
Silvery sparkly
Stars in the moonlight
Moving.

Umehra Khalid (8)
Wakefield Girls' High School, Wakefield

Young Writers - A Pocketful Of Rhyme West Yorkshire

Go And Open The Door

(Based on 'The Door' by Miroslav Holub)

Go and open the door,
Maybe outside there's a silver bird gliding and
Swooping in the sky,
Or a golden tree with wings like lightning.

Maybe there is a golden shadow glittering in the
Light blue sea,
Or a singing robin bathing in a bird bath.

Maybe there are little pink bunnies hopping
Cheerfully to their burrows,
Or maybe there is a large fish buying sunshades.

Maybe there are stars glistening in the moonlit sky,
Or a child singing as sweet as a baby.

Eleanor Westwood (8)
Wakefield Girls' High School, Wakefield

The Open Door

(Based on 'The Door' by Miroslav Holub)

Go and open the door
Maybe outside there is
A heap of snow
Higher than the house
Ready for you to jump in.

Maybe there is
A land made out of gold
With gleaming diamonds.

Maybe there is
A garden made of chocolate
With magical animals
Which play all day.

Maybe there is
A pink sun glistening
In the sky
All day long.

Emma Cox (9)
Wakefield Girls' High School, Wakefield

If I Weren't Me

If I were an animal I would be a
White Shetland pony
Running gracefully in a green field.

If I were a bird I would be a
Small blue tit
Singing gently in the sunset sky.

If I were a piece of furniture I would be a
Soft pink sofa with white cushions
In a cosy room with a real fire.

If you could eat me I would be
Yummy crispy chips
In a burning hot pan.

If I were the most famous person
I would be Kylie
Singing in a concert.

If I were the weather I would be
The golden shining sun
In the pale blue sky.

I like being me because
I am alive and I am special.

Beatrice Marshall-Hodson (9)
Wakefield Girls' High School, Wakefield

My Brother

My brother's very annoying,
He steals all my toys,
He hits me with his golf stick,
And makes me hang out with nursery boys.

Still I have to play with him,
Even though he is a pest,
He comes and says, 'Please play with me,'
Even when I am revising for a test.

I want to know why they don't listen, maybe it's because
They think he's a pearl,
But still I keep wondering
Why didn't we have a girl?

He ruins my clothes
And breaks all my toys,
He makes me watch CBeebies and silly DVDs
He also makes loads of noise.

Yet no matter what he does
I still love him so,
No other brother could ever replace him,
Because he's my little bro.

Kathryn Marwood (9)
Wakefield Girls' High School, Wakefield

A Monster

He starts his day, a bit grumpy,
Falling out of his bed, a bit bumpy,
Scratching his head, hearing strange noises,
He thinks he is hearing voices,
But it's him just yawning and growling,
As he is getting ready to go prowling.

He's a bit clumsy and very big,
Smelly, spotty and hairy like a pig,
He has teeth made up of fangs,
He walks with a thump and plenty of bangs.

He's not the quietest of monsters but the loudest,
And seems to be the scariest,
But guess what, we all like him,
He helps the people and he's not dim,
Cute, clever and very kind,
We've made up our mind,
We love our monster!

Moneek Chahal (9)
Wakefield Girls' High School, Wakefield

Pretty Ponies

Pretty ponies prance around the green, grassy field,
Their sleek, silky coats shine in the sun.
Pretty ponies parade in the delightful dressage,
Their shiny saddles and beautiful bridles.
Pretty ponies play with the tug-toys in their stables,
They whinny, whine and whisper to each other all the noisy night.
Pretty ponies paw at the dusty, dirty ground,
They look for their favourite, final feed.
Pretty ponies promise to give their racing riders,
A rocketing, rapid ride
On super stallions,
Gorgeous geldings,
And marvellous mares.

Amelia Dobson (8)
Wakefield Girls' High School, Wakefield

My Dog

They say a dog is a Man's best friend
Loving and loyal until the end,
This must be true
As my dog simply loves me and you.

When my dog has puppies, I will not give them away
Even if someone wants to buy them I will not let them pay
He is fluffy, puffy and simply mad
That's why I feel so lucky especially when I am sad.

To have a silent furry friend to talk to and stroke
As he cannot talk back, but he likes to joke
When my dog chews on my lace, and makes them tear
He gets in everybody's hair.

His face is so cute and makes me laugh
Oh what fun we have in the bath
Suds and bubbles in the air
What a mess, my parents would go spare.

When I hear my dog scratch on the door
I hate it because I say stop but he scratches more
Everyone knows that dogs run really fast
So in a race I will come last.

When my dog and I go out for a run
My dog and I come back all full of fun
I really hate it when his paws are really mucky
But at least he's a playful puppy.

On a rainy day when I open my umbrella
My dog runs down to the cellar
In the middle of the night when it is dark
My dog if it hears a sound will definitely bark.

Evangelina Fozard (9)
Wakefield Girls' High School, Wakefield

What Am I?

I am sly not timid,
Furry not tame,
Sneaky and chatty,
I growl and I screech,
And I hunt all night long,
I am strong with all my powers of my sneakiness,
I growl through the night and sleep through the day,
My brown bushy tail with dots of red and white,
I open up my mouth to take a big bite.

What am I?

Amy Rolinson (8)
Wakefield Girls' High School, Wakefield

In The Dark

You can see someone's shadow
You can see someone outside
You can see someone lurking in the corner
You can see someone under your bed
You can see someone in a bush
You can see someone hiding in the wardrobe.

You can hear the gravel crunching outside
You can hear the owls hooting
You can hear the footsteps of a monster
You can hear the ghost wail down the hall
You can hear the dogs howl
You can hear the trees scratch the window.

You feel someone is watching you
You feel someone is following you
You feel someone is ready to pounce on you
You feel someone's hot breath on your neck
You feel someone at the end of your bed
You feel the sun breaking out.

Charlotte Lupton (8)
Wakefield Girls' High School, Wakefield

The Ocean

I am a greenish blue colour,
I am very, very deep,
There are lots of different kinds of creatures in my belly,
But when you smell things in me I can be very, very smelly,
People often visit to swim or just to see me,
I am very big and very wide,
If I get angry I splash about,
But if I am calm I stay still,
I carry along boats for a ride,
I taste salty and cold,
I am very big and very, very great.

What am I?

Jennifer Selim (8)
Wakefield Girls' High School, Wakefield

Footballs

Footballs are fat but they don't bounce on a mat,
They are black and white,
Spotty and dotty,
Footballs are round,
But if you lose them they are not easily found,
Footballs are fat,
They are also thin,
But some footballs are light
Some footballs are heavy,
Some people are silly,
And call their footballs Milly
But I am not silly
And I don't call my football Milly
I just kick it around.

Jessica Holland (9)
Wakefield Girls' High School, Wakefield

Teddy Bears

Teddy bears are friendly things
Never complain or whine,
Just sit there trying to comfort you,
Whilst their hazelnut eyes shine.

When you're sad and lonely,
Just look around your bed,
And I'll be there waiting for you,
Me, your old friend Ted.

Caitlin Halliday (9)
Wakefield Girls' High School, Wakefield

Tiger

I crawled, cautiously and carefully through the jungle,
Putting down each padded paw as quietly as could be,
My sleek body, climbed upon trees and ducked under branches,
Camouflaged and silent,
Waiting to pounce on my unsuspecting prey,
To tear it apart and sink my teeth into the tender flesh.

But now, I pace up and down my cold, hard prison,
Captured and stared at by passers-by,
My daily meat is brought to my cage.
Fat, lazy and bored,
I chase birds, butterflies and my own tail.
Or lay on the artificial rock,
Put there to make me feel at home.

But when I sleep, I am back in the thick jungle,
I hear the monkeys chattering high above me,
I feel the damp, green leaves beneath my padded paws
And the tropical rain falling on my striped back.
I feel alive again, a proud, majestic creature.

Claudia Lindley (9)
Wakefield Girls' High School, Wakefield

Cats

Cats can be fat and do nothing at all,
Some can be thin and walk on the wall.
Cats can eat salmon and Parma ham,
Some cats can eat as little as they can.
Cats can have a collar pink or black,
Some can have leaves upon their back.
Cats know how to put up a fight,
Even if they can read and write.
Cats know what they want to do,
But sometimes they do not have a clue!
Cats purr by the fire, flaming gold,
But they never seem to do what they're told!

Kate Wilding (9)
Wakefield Girls' High School, Wakefield

A Vampire

I have a white face and bright red lips
I have sharp white fangs
I wear a massive black cloak,
I sneak up on you when it's really dark,
I suck people's red blood,
People dress up as me when it is Hallowe'en.
I can also transform into a scary bat.

What am I?

Sneeha Lal (9)
Wakefield Girls' High School, Wakefield

A Rose

My stalk is jungle green and brown,
And I grow through the moist ground.

Some people say I'm flattering,
Others say I'm dazzling.

Some say I'm pretty and beautifully pink,
And even sometimes the colour of ink.

You give me to someone on Valentine's Day,
And you like to dance with me on a gorgeous day.

What am I?

Ellie Spruce (8)
Wakefield Girls' High School, Wakefield

My Dad

My dad's chubby, but funny,
He's going bald but staying bold,
He feels like a big fluffy teddy bear
Who hardly has any hair,
He buys me things,
Like golden rings.
He isn't very tight,
When he kisses me goodnight.
He is my best friend,
My love for him will never end.

Gemma Green (9)
Wakefield Girls' High School, Wakefield

My Big Brother

My brother can be a bully
My brother teases me
My brother likes to have a fight
But he never ever bites.

My brother hides my homework
My brother can be really mean
My brother can hate me so
But really, he is not my foe.

My brother thinks he is the best
My brother is sooo tall
My brother is like an annoying bee
But when I'm hurt he looks after me.

My brother gets to stay up late
My brother shouts at me
My brother always does things first
But I love him so much I could burst.

Rebecca Jessop (9)
Wakefield Girls' High School, Wakefield

Teachers

Teachers can be tall
Teachers can be small
Some teachers have no fashion sense
But some go to the mall
Teachers can be fat
Teachers can be thin
Some are good at losing
But others like to win
Teachers can be active
Teachers can be lazy
Some are very accurate
But others can be hazy
Teachers can be loud
Teachers can be quiet
Some stay sitting
But others run riot.

Lydia Jenkinson (9)
Wakefield Girls' High School, Wakefield

A Vampire

I am very scary,
I have long red nails,
My fingers are really long.
I am medium size and
Have got smooth skin.
I can be sneaky at times.
I am really dangerous,
I have long sharp teeth,
Which are sparkling white.
I drink lots of blood
Especially humans' blood.

What am I?

Rachael Dent (9)
Wakefield Girls' High School, Wakefield

Dancing

At dancing there is lots of fun
And lots of work to be done.
A pas de chat is a step of a cat,
It's really hard if you are fat.

A pirouette goes round and round
And makes you dizzy, hit the ground.
Those that practise make it work,
If you saw me you would go berserk.

Charlotte Sobota (8)
Wakefield Girls' High School, Wakefield

Fairy-Tale Game

Bones and treasure, armour and swords
In the castle, don't ignore
Dragons and ogres, monsters and all
Follow inside; take a look, there is lots more.
A princess locked up inside a room
In the tallest tower near the moon
A handsome prince comes riding by
He rescues her from the scary night
But help, look out, duck, there is fire
The dragon has seen them
Quick they must hurry down the steps, through the door
Get out! Get out! Before there is more
Once again on the other side
We say goodbye to this fairy-tale life
Night night ogres, dragons, knights and damsels
As I turn off the game and get into bed
It is time to rest my weary head
Until tomorrow when I turn the page
I dream again of the next stage.

Eve Johnston (9)
Wakefield Girls' High School, Wakefield

School

School is very exciting,
Though it might not seem so,
With all the tests and writing,
And lift up desk lids too.

School is very fun,
In every different way,
With all the different topics,
That you can learn and play.

School is very good,
It gives you education,
And helps you learn more things,
Than you already know.

School is very lovely,
For in spring all its blossom trees,
Are lovely as can be,
They are always scattered around the playground,
So that we can see them clearly as can be.

Lucie Harrison (9)
Wakefield Girls' High School, Wakefield

Stars

Stars so light
Stars so bright
Please give me my wish
That I wish tonight.

I sit here so lonely
And so very sad

So give me my wish
That I wish tonight.

I look really closely
And I see a star
All different from all the others
It's bright, twinkling, glitters in the sky
So give me my wish
That I wish tonight.

I see a dying star
5000 light years away
I wish upon that special little star
That I look at each night
So give me my wish
That I wish tonight.

Megan Cowley (9)
Wakefield Girls' High School, Wakefield